Look at Me!

by John Serrano

Look at me! I have a skateboard.

I like to ride my skateboard.

Look at me! I like to ride.
I have a new bike. I have
a helmet, too.

Look at me! I play soccer.

I am good at soccer.

Look at me! I like to read books.

I am a good reader!

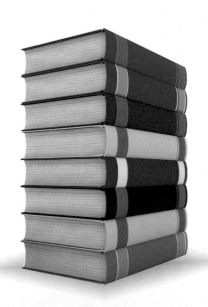

Look at me! I play the guitar.

I like to play.

Look at me! I play basketball.
I am good at basketball. I play
in my wheelchair.

Look at me! I like to dance.

I can dance on my toes.

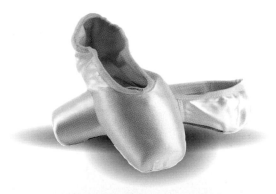

Look at me!